BIRD
HABITATS &
CONSERVATION

David Chandler and Mike Langman
Introduction by Bill Oddie

HAMLYN

To Tanya, Rebecca and Adam.

WEST GRID STAMP

NN		RR		WW	
NT		RT		WO	
NC		RC		WL	
NH		RB		WM	
NL		RP		WT	
NV		RS		WA	
NM		RW		WR	
NB		RV		WS	
NE					
NP					

First published in 1995 by Hamlyn
an imprint of Reed Consumer Books Limited
Michelin House, 81 Fulham Road, London SW3 6RB
and Auckland, Melbourne, Singapore and Toronto.

Copyright © Reed International Books Limited 1995

Text copyright © David Chandler 1995
Illustrations copyright © Mike Langman 1995
Photographs copyright © see page 48.

ISBN 0 600 57982 4

A CIP catalogue record for this book is available from
the British Library.

Cover photograph: Puffin © Colin Carver (Nature
Photographers Limited)
Back cover photograph: © David Chandler
Printed and bound in Hong Kong

CONTENTS

BILL ODDIE'S INTRODUCTION

Grown ups love droning on about how different – and difficult – things were when they were young. Well, when it comes to bird watching ... it's true! I was about seven when I managed to persuade my dad to buy me my first pair of binoculars. That was over 40 years ago, and there weren't any bird magazines of specialist optical dealers. I was lucky I didn't end up with a plastic toy pair! In fact, my first binoculars were very good and lasted for years, so dad must have taken good advice from somewhere.

But how did I get help about how and where to go bird-watching? And how did I know what I was looking at? The only identification book available was the *Observer's Book of Birds*, which didn't even have all the British species in it, let alone pictures of them in all their plumages. The first 'modern' field guide came out in 1954 when I was 13.

I like to think, though, that by the time I became a teenager I wasn't a bad birder. So, how did I do it? Well, nearly every day, I used to walk to the local woods and around the golf course (watching out for flying balls as well as birds). Every weekend, I'd cycle to the local reservoir or persuade my dad to give me a lift. And I'd campaign to take our family holidays in Norfolk or Devon so that I could see some new species. I spent an amazing amount of time but, looking back, I probably wasted a lot too, making mistakes I could have avoided if only there'd been books like this one.

This book deals with Habitats and Conservation. When I was a lad, these were words I didn't know the meaning of. Nowadays, everyone is far more aware of environmental problems. It is knowledge that we simply must use if we are to preserve the world and its wildlife (including birds and ourselves). However, the truth is, although young people may be well informed, it's the adults that are 'in charge'. What's more, I'm willing to bet that this book contains lots of information that most adults don't know. So PASS IT ON!

Yes, things have changed – and not all for the better – but the fact that more and more birdwatchers are now also con-servationists has to be a good thing. I also believe that study-ing habitats and conservation makes a wonderful hobby even more fascinating and truly important. Birdwatching is an interest for life. I'm still at it. Never give it up.

Bill Oddie

INTRODUCTION

I grew up on the edge of London and spent most of my spare time on wasteland not far from where I lived, where there were fields, hedges, streams and patches of woodland. To me it was a wilderness, and it was where I discovered herons, grey wagtails, great spotted woodpeckers and foxes.

For years there had been plans to build a by-pass across my wilderness. With a friend I collected signatures from over 200 local people who said they agreed with us – they did not want to lose the area or its wildlife. We sent the signatures to the council, but we lost the battle. Since then, the road has been built. There is one dead tree there that I can still recognise, but everything else has gone.

When I was a teenager in the 1980's, I worked as a volunteer on some nature reserves. One of the birds I saw was the red-backed shrike. It was quite easy to see, but less than ten years later they were extinct as a breeding bird in the UK. A few years later I was lucky enough to work on some wonderful Scottish islands – the Outer Hebrides. Sometimes, we were kept awake at night by corncrakes calling right outside the window. Today, corncrakes are threatened with worldwide extinction.

I have seen these things happen in my own lifetime, and I am not that old! People need wildlife, but sadly, the world's wildlife is facing some serious threats. Read on and find out some of the facts for yourself. And, when you have read the book, please do me a favour: make sure that you do your bit for the world's birds. You <u>can</u> help to make a difference.

David Chandler

My wilderness today: a busy dual-carriageway by-passing a London suburb.

GOING, GOING, GONE

The passenger pigeon was the commonest bird that ever lived. Just 200 years ago there were between 5,000 and 10,000 million in North America but, by 1900, they were extinct in the wild. In under 100 years they had been completely wiped out.

Big passenger pigeon flocks were three or four miles wide and 300 miles long! In 1813, John Audubon, a famous American ornithologist, watched a flock fly past; it took three days! At times, he guessed that 1,000 million birds were passing by in just a few hours. Scientist Alexander Wilson estimated 2000 million pigeons in a flock that he had seen.

The pigeons used to feed, nest and roost in huge groups and there are stories of branches, even whole trees, collapsing under the weight of roosting birds. How could a bird that was so numerous disappear in such a short period of time?

After 80 years, and with human help, white-tailed eagles are breeding in the wild again in Britain.

Passenger pigeons were hunted for food for many years. As the number of people increased, so did the demand for pigeon meat. Lots of birds could be knocked out of the air just by waving a stick around, and professional trappers developed more and more efficient ways to catch pigeons. Roosting trees were felled; pigeons were gassed by burning grass or sulphur; and one shot from a shotgun could kill 100 birds. One trapper caught 24,000 birds in ten days and, at one cent per pigeon, he made $240 which was a lot of money 100 years ago.

In the 1880's, people noticed that there were fewer passenger pigeons around. Laws were introduced to control the trappers, but these were not enforced and the numbers of pigeons carried on falling. Between 1910 and 1912, rewards were offered for anyone who saw a wild passenger pigeon. But it was too late. They were extinct in the wild. The last surviving passenger pigeon died in Cincinnati Zoo in 1914.

Trapping was probably not the only cause of the passenger pigeons extinction. Today, we know that some birds which breed in colonies raise more young per pair in large colonies than in small ones. Trapping probably reduced the pigeon numbers so much that they were unable to breed successfully. They were dying faster than they could raise young, so there was no way the species could survive.

We still have not learnt our lesson. Today, there are still many birds that are in danger of disappearing forever. Of the 9,700 species of birds in the world, over 1,100 are threatened with extinction. And this is not restricted to exotic birds in faraway places. The white-tailed eagle used

to be widespread throughout the British Isles; it even used to breed as far south as the Isle of Wight. The last British pair tried to breed on Skye, in Scotland, in 1916.

Their decline began in the 1600s. Like many birds of prey, they were killed because people thought they were pests. Some sheep farmers believed the eagles ate new born lambs and so they destroyed as many of the eagles as possible. As white-tailed eagles became rarer, they also became highly prized by animal collectors who wanted stuffed white-tailed eagles and eggs.

More recently, pesticides almost wiped out the white-tailed eagle in Europe. Pesticides built up at the top of the food chain killing adult eagles. They also caused the birds to lay eggs with shells so thin that they broke when the adult tried to incubate them.

Passenger pigeon flocks were so big that they took days to fly by. Today, this species is extinct.

Thankfully, unlike the passenger pigeon, there is still hope for the white-tailed eagle. In Norway, there are at least 1500 pairs and the population is growing. Since 1975, a small number of these Scandinavian eagles have been released on Rum, a rocky Scottish island. Eighty two birds were released in the first 11 years and, in 1982, a pair began to build a nest. In 1985, one pair bred successfully and became the first white-tailed eagles to breed in the British Isles for 70 years. The white-tailed eagle was back! In 1994, there were four pairs living in the wild in Britain and five young were raised.

The future of the white-tailed eagle in the UK is still not certain, but there is hope.

Today, habitat loss is the biggest threat facing the world's birds. Uplands are just one of the habitats humans have damaged. Some moorlands (right) have been ploughed up with heavy machinery to make way for huge plantations of conifers.

HABITATS AT RISK

A habitat is the name given to the place where a plant or animal lives. Woodland, heathland and moorland are all examples of wildlife habitats. The British Isles have a variety of habitats, each with its own bird community.

The skylark (above) is a farmland bird, but there are fewer than there used to be.

Gardens and parks

Over 50 bird species can be seen in gardens and parks. When a bird sees a garden from the air it looks like open woodland with trees, shrubs and grassy areas. It is not surprising then, that many garden birds were originally woodland birds which have learnt to cope with people.

The natural food and shelter provided by gardens is tempting enough, but when extra bird food is provided, gardens must be irresistible! In woods, blue tits eat aphids, caterpillars and seeds, but in gardens, nuts are definitely their favourite. If you spread old apples on the lawn in winter, you could see redwings and fieldfares; hang up some bacon rinds and you might be lucky enough to be visited by a great spotted woodpecker.

Sparrowhawks are becoming more common in town gardens. You might not like the thought of a sparrowhawk eating a tit or finch that was feeding in your garden but the sparrowhawk has to eat, too! The number of small birds in an area will determine how many sparrowhawks there are, not the other way round. If you see a sparrowhawk, it is a sign of a healthy bird population.

However, the song thrush, a common garden bird, is having problems. The population has gone down over recent years, probably because of changes in the way Britain's countryside is looked after.

Farmland

Seventy five per cent of Britain is farmland – from hill-top sheep farming to intensive cereal-growing. Some farmland provides good wildlife habitat, but a lot is not as wildlife friendly as it used to be.

Farms with lots of hedges (above right) are good for wildlife. If the hedges are ripped out, what is left is a wildlife desert.

Good farms for wildlife are those with ponds, hedges and other habitats. Ponds used to be common on sheep and cattle farms; they were the only way to provide water for the livestock. Mallards, sedge warblers and moorhens all nested around farm ponds. Today, many ponds have been neglected and are overgrown with plants. They have been replaced with water pipes and troughs which are easier to look after, but attract little wildlife.

Hedges are the traditional way of keeping animals in the right field and of marking the boundary between one farm and the next. Many are hundreds of years old, some are over a thousand. From a bird's point of view, the taller and wider a hedge, and the more types of tree and shrub in it, the better.

Since 1984, over 100,000 miles of hedgerow have been lost through neglect and because they take up space that could be grazed or used for growing crops. Hedges also get in the way of the big machinery used on modern farms. As well as hedges disappearing, rough grassland around many field edges has been ploughed up. This grassland used to support the voles which barn owls eat. Now barn owls in these areas have to look along roadside verges for voles and some are killed by traffic.

The government now realises that farmers in Britain are growing more food than we need and they are encouraging farmers to do things differently. Hedges, trees and wild flowers are being planted and fields left empty in winter rather than being planted with winter crops. This is good news for farmland wildlife

Woodlands

Deciduous woods (where trees lose their leaves in the autumn) are normally better for birds than coniferous woods. Woods with lots of oak trees are especially good because they support huge numbers of invertebrates. The best woods have plenty of dead tree, too. Great spotted woodpeckers feed on the insect larvae that bore into rotting wood. Nuthatches, woodpeckers and tits all nest in holes and dead trees are perfect for this.

Woods have been managed by humans for a long time. Many trees regrow into straight, slender poles after they are cut down and these trees were managed by cutting them in turn in different parts of a wood (coppicing). Coppiced woods are good for wildlife: the opened areas let in light so plants and insects thrive.

Coniferous woods are mostly man-made plantations – they are timber farms and wood is the crop. They are not as good for birds as deciduous woods because they are less varied and very dark so few plants can grow. Newly-planted forests are better than older forests. These are good for nightjars, black grouse, hen harriers and woodlarks. By the time the trees are 15 years old the woods are thick and dark and fewer birds can live in them.

Caledonian pine forest is Britain's only natural coniferous forest and it is a very important wildlife habitat. It is

Healthy lowland rivers are beautiful and support plenty of wildlife, such as kingfishers.

found in the Scottish Highlands and is home to special birds like capercaillies, Scottish crossbills and crested tits. Unfortunately, deer eat the young trees in these natural forests, which means that there are few trees to take over when the old pines die.

Only a few woods have been lost in Britain in the last 15 years. More woods are being coppiced and plantations are being improved for wildlife. Most of Britain's woodland is not under serious threat, and conservationists are doing all they can to save the Caledonian pine forest.

Streams and rivers

Mountain streams are shallow and clear; they bubble and crash over rocks and boulders. If you are lucky, you'll see a remarkable bird which lives near fast-flowing water – a dipper. These birds are chocolate-brown with white chests and they bob up and down. Their feathers are thick and soft to keep them warm in the cold mountain waters.

They need to be because dippers find their insect food by 'flying' underwater.

Goosanders live further down mountains than dippers. The goosander's bill has edges like a saw to keep hold of slippery fish. Their nesting place is unusual for a duck: they nest in holes in hollow trees!

Down in the lowlands, rivers wind slowly across the countryside getting deeper and wider, and the water is not very clear because it carries more mud. Mute swans and mallards are common; kingfishers and sand martins could be nesting, and lush vegetation provides moorhens with ideal nesting places. If there are reeds along the riverbank, there could be reed warblers and sedge warblers, which often breed in tangles of riverside plants.

Our waterways face an invisible hazard. Nitrates and phosphates from fertilizers run off fields into rivers. Sewage ends up in rivers, too, and can also contain nitrates and phosphates. This blast of nutrients makes the river plants grow too quickly. They soon die and decompose in the water (a process called eutrophication) and little, if any, oxygen is left. The river then smells awful and is almost lifeless.

Scientists have also found that where water runs through newly planted conifer plantations into rivers, the rivers are more acidic than normal. This causes the number of invertebrates, which are food for birds like dippers, to drop. And, if one part of the food web suffers, other parts will, too.

Common woodland birds (from left): a jay, a green woodpecker feeding on the ground, a nuthatch, long-tailed tits foraging, a wren, a blackcap, a tawny owl roosting and a sparrowhawk hunting.

Lakes

A lake's wildlife depends on its water quality. Most lakes in northern England and lochs in Scotland are 'oligotrophic': they contain acidic water and few nutrients. They support few plants, few invertebrates and few birds.

However, what they lack in quantity they make up for in quality. Some of our rarest birds, including black-throated and red-throated divers and nearly all of Britain's ospreys breed on or around these lakes. And, in winter, whooper swans and wild geese roost on them.

Other lakes contain alkaline water with lots of nutrients. These lakes are called 'eutrophic' and they support a wider variety of wildlife. They provide a good breeding habitat for grebes, grey herons, mute swans, Canada geese, ducks, coots and water rails. Ducks, grebes, coots and gulls depend on these lakes in winter.

There are not many natural eutrophic lakes left, but there are a lot of man-made ones. Gravel pits are eutrophic lakes with their own special characteristics. They are shallower, muddier and more varied so they attract a good variety of birds. One or two

The bittern is the rarest bird to breed regularly in Britain. The species cannot survive without reedbeds.

species are gravel pit specialities. The little ringed plover bred in Britain just over 50 years ago for the first time. Now, there are over 600 pairs. Elsewhere, they breed on stony river beds, but in Britain, they nest on similar areas around gravel pits.

As well as the threat of pollution, gravel pit birds have to cope with disturbance. People sail, water ski and jet ski on pits and this can disturb birds – breeding birds might desert their nests and wintering birds waste valuable energy every time they are forced to fly.

One solution is zoning. More and more gravel pits are divided into different zones:

Gravel pits can be excellent places to watch birds. From left: a kingfisher, a little grebe, roosting mallards, a great crested grebe family, coots, black-headed gulls, a Canada goose family and a moorhen.

A wet grassland. From left: a yellow wagtail, two redshanks (one taking flight), two lapwings (one in the air), a snipe and reed buntings.

one area becomes a nature reserve, another is for water sports. This keeps most people happy and means that the wildlife is not disturbed as much.

Reedbeds

The bittern is one of the rarest breeding birds in Britain and it spends most of its life in reedbeds. Bearded tits also depend on reedbeds for a place to breed and for insects to eat in summer and reed seeds in winter. Reedbeds also provide safe nesting places for birds such as marsh harriers, water rails, reed warblers and sedge warblers.

Many reedbeds have been damaged because they have not been properly looked after. They need to be wet and the best ones are cut regularly to stop the bed from drying out. This stops other plants from growing, drying out the bed, and taking over from the reeds. The few big reedbeds left in Britain are now mostly in the care of conservation organisations.

Wet grasslands

Traditionally grazed by sheep and cattle and used for hay making, wet grasslands are special places for wildlife.

Over the years, however, many have been drained to make them easier to farm.

Those that are farmed in the traditional way are important breeding and wintering areas, especially for waders and wildfowl. The Ouse Washes in East Anglia is a good example. Redshanks, snipe, lapwings, mallards, tufted ducks, gadwalls, and shovelers all breed there, as well as rarer birds like black tailed godwits, ruffs and garganeys. In the autumn tens of thousands of swans and ducks arrive for winter.

Like reed beds, wet grasslands need to be kept wet. One of the best ways to do this is to use cattle and sheep as mowing machines. This stops trees taking over and produces short and long grass. Different birds prefer different lengths – lapwings and godwits breed in areas with short grass, tufted ducks and gadwalls prefer longer grass.

The Ouse Washes have been protected as a nature reserve for over 20 years. Other wet grasslands could still be drained and lost.

Artificial islands on gravel pits and reservoirs encourage common terns (above) to breed.

13

Hills and mountains

The hills and mountains (uplands) of the British Isles include some of its wildest places. Uplands have three things in common: poor soil, low temperatures and lots of rain (or snow). The higher you go, the more it rains, the colder it is and the poorer the soil. Wild mountain tops have very little soil because it is washed or blown away. This means that there are few plants; few plants means there are few birds.

On flatter mountain ridges, which are covered in snow for long periods, there is more soil and so there are more plants and birds. This habitat is a bit like Arctic tundra and is home to some remarkable birds:

■ The ptarmigan is a mountain-top grouse. It is mostly brown in summer but white in winter for camouflage.

■ The dotterel is a high altitude wader and is unusual because the female's markings are brighter than the male's. The male does most of the egg incubation and looks after the young.

■ The snow bunting is a truly Arctic bird. It breeds nearer to the North Pole than any other small bird. A few pairs sometimes breed in wild mountain areas in the British Isles.

Many of our wildest mountains are almost untouched by humans, but there are still threats. The ski industry wants to build more ski runs and walkers sometimes disturb breeding birds.

More types of plants grow on the lower hills and there is a greater variety of birds. Many hills are important breeding areas for hen harriers, merlins, short-eared owls, red and black grouse, curlews, snipe, golden plovers, greenshanks and dunlins.

Hills might look wild but most have been managed by humans for hundreds of years. Today on the hills, people rear grouse for shooting, stalk deer and graze sheep. Sheep grazing can cause problems for wildlife: where there are too many sheep, areas which were covered in heather are being overgrazed and these special wildlife areas are turning into rough grassland.

Rocky coasts and the sea

The UK has 11,000 miles of coastline and is one of the north Atlantic's most important seabird stations. The gannet, famous for its spectacular 60 mph plunge dives, is a species which depends on our coast: over 70 per cent of all the world's gannets breed in less than 20 colonies around Britain.

In the breeding season, a seabird colony is alive with thousands of birds. Fulmars, kitti-wakes, razorbills, guillemots,

A Scottish mountain top with a raven flying high, a golden eagle, and a ptarmigan and a female dotterel in their summer plumages.

puffins, shags and cormorants nest close to each other. It is noisy, busy and often extremely smelly! But most of these birds spend only a small part of their lives on the cliff. Most of the year they are at sea and when they come to land to breed, they still have to go to sea to find food.

Humans treat the sea like a massive rubbish dump. Every day, 300 million gallons of sewage, thousands of tonnes of metals and nitrates are dumped in the sea. Nobody knows what effect this is having on the marine food web.

One oil spill in the wrong place at the wrong time could be disastrous for a seabird colony. One million tonnes of oil from ships and oil platforms finds its way into the North Sea every year, and that doesn't include accidental spills.

European fishing methods are now so efficient that a quarter to a half of all the North Sea's fish are caught every year. We compete with wildlife for fish and, at the moment, the wildlife is losing. We are taking too many fish.

So far, our seabird populations do not seem to be too badly affected, but we have to sort out the problems before it is too late. We need:

1. More Marine Nature Reserves – currently, there are only two and this isn't enough. The most important sea areas must be made into Marine Nature Reserves as soon as possible.

2. Safe routes for ships – routes that steer ships away from important wildlife areas to protect them from pollution and disturbance.

3. Proper waste disposal – ports need easy-to-use waste disposal facilities so that ships have no excuse for dumping their waste at sea.

4. To catch less fish! At the moment, there are not enough fish to go round. If fish are taken out of the sea faster than they can breed, their numbers will go down and, eventually, there will be no fish left – a disaster for seabirds and fishermen. Get this one right and it will be good news for birds and people.

A bustling seabird colony packed with fulmars, gannets, kittiwakes, shags, guillemots, razorbills and puffins.

Estuaries

Estuaries are where rivers meet the sea. The tide comes in and goes out twice a day, mixing fresh river water with salty sea water. From a bird's point of view, the best thing about an estuary is the mud. At high tide, the mud is covered, but when the tide is out the food-rich mudflats provide a banquet for many wading birds.

Britain's estuaries provide food and shelter for up to one and a half million wading birds each winter; that's 40 per cent of the total number in north-west Europe. One large estuary, the Wash on the east coast of England, supports a quarter of all the knots which breed in Greenland and Canada.

Estuary mud is home to millions of invertebrates. There are few invertebrate species that can cope with the changing saltiness, but those that can live there in huge numbers. Over 2000 Corophium (a small shrimp) and Hydrobia (a tiny snail) have been

If waders such as these knots, are disturbed, they are forced to fly and use up valuable energy.

counted in an area of estuary mud the size of these two pages, To a dunlin or redshank, this is the energy equivalent of one and a half Mars bars!

East Atlantic Flyway

The East Atlantic Flyway stretches from Arctic Canada, Greenland and Siberia down over western Europe to South Africa. It is one of the world's great migration routes and British estuaries form an essential part of it.

Every autumn, five or six million waders and wildfowl travel along the flyway. About two million spend the winter on British estuaries and the others use them for resting and refuelling (stuffing themselves with invertebrates to build up their energy stores before heading farther south). If these birds did not stop to rest and feed, they would not reach their destinations.

Estuaries are important for other birds, too. Sea-going ducks like scoters, long-tailed ducks and eiders shelter during rough weather and they provide food for small birds like finches, larks, pipits and buntings in winter. These small birds are hunted by merlins and sparrowhawks. Hen harriers and short-eared owls also hunt over estuaries for small mammals and birds.

Winter isn't the only time estuaries are used by birds: 20,000 pairs of redshanks nest in the marshy areas around estuaries. (Only 35,000 pairs breed in the British Isles.)

It is not difficult to see how important estuaries are for birds, but they have a lot to offer people too, and this sometimes causes problems for wildlife.

Estuaries are beautiful, wild places but not everyone sees it that way. Some people

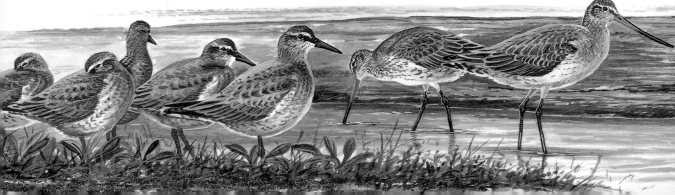

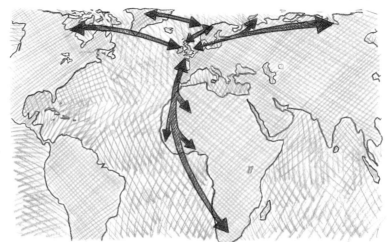

The East Atlantic Flyway (right) is a major migration route. After breeding in the Arctic, millions of birds use Britain's estuaries for feeding and resting on their way farther south.

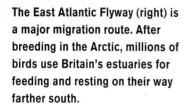

Estuary birds (below left to right): knots, bar-tailed godwits, dunlins, an oystercatcher, redshanks, a curlew, a shelduck and a grey heron. Dunlins in flight (above).

think that they are ugly, muddy places and would like to improve them by building a barrage and covering all the mud with a big artificial lake. When barrages are built, birds lose out. Large areas of food-rich mud are covered with water and important feeding areas are lost.

Some barrages are designed to turn the power of the sea's tides into electricity. Others act like dams and stop estuary water flowing into the sea. The lakes created behind the barrages are used for sailing, jet skiing and windsurfing.

Many estuaries face a number of small threats rather than one big one. Mudflats are drained here and there so that they can be farmed or built on. Sewage, fertilizers, pesticides, chemicals from factories and oil all

pollute the water. Modern machines dig up shellfish, removing wildlife food and disturbing the birds. Large shellfish farms stop birds feeding. Marinas are built on precious mudflats. Boats, wind-surfers and even bird-watchers disturb feeding, nesting and roosting birds, forcing them to fly and use up valuable energy.

Migrating birds using the East Atlantic Flyway need our estuaries. On many estuaries, there is room for people and wildlife. We have to make sure that building, sailing and all other human activities take place where they will not disturb wildlife and leave some special areas for birds.

Heaths

Heaths are found in a handful of countries in north-west Europe. In all of these countries, huge areas of heathland have been lost. In Britain alone, over 70 per cent has disappeared since 1830; the Netherlands has lost 95 per cent of it's heathland and figures from Sweden and Denmark are just as worrying.

Like much of Britain, heathlands used to be woodland. When the trees were cleared by humans, the water and the nutrients drained deep into the soil and few plants could survive. One plant that could survive, however, was heather.

On a few heathlands, heather is almost the only plant species, but most have a few others, as well. Normally, heaths have some clumps of thick, prickly gorse and a few birch or pine trees. Because there aren't many different types of plants, there are few species of insects and only a few birds. The birds that can make a living on heaths live there in small numbers, but most are very special species.

One special heathland bird is the Dartford warbler. Most British warblers spend the winter in Africa or the Mediterranean. The Dartford warbler is unusual because it doesn't migrate. It spends the whole year on heathland. The Dartford warbler is a handsome, active bird with a long, flicking tail. It nests in clumps of gorse where it finds its food of insects and spiders. Spending the whole year in Britain can be risky – during cold winters the numbers of Dartford warblers can drop very quickly. Normally, as long as there are a few mild winters, the numbers go up again.

There is more life on the heath in the summer. Hobbys, falcons which visit Britain for the warmer months, dash through the air picking off dragonflies. At night, another agile insect-eating bird comes out; the nightjar. This is a superbly camouflaged bird which spends the daytime lying low on the ground. But when the sun goes down, the nightjar gets up. The perching male sings his strange churring song. When he stops churring he is probably hunting. His flight is fast and silent and he has a big mouth – ideal for grabbing moths and beetles.

Heathlands with ponds are also important for dragonflies, and all six British reptiles are found on the heaths in southern England. The smooth snake and the sand lizard are both found only in Britain and depend on heathland.

Heathland wildlife, from left to right: a Dartford warbler, a hobby, a stonechat, a dragonfly, a sand lizard and a smooth snake.

Young birch and pine trees are pulled up to stop them taking over a heath.

New housing estates are destroying some British heathlands.

Heathlands are not a natural habitat. If they had been left alone, birch and pine trees would have started to grow and more water and nutrients would be held in the soil: eventually, most heaths would turn into woodland. It is only man's activities that have stopped this happening. Traditionally, cattle, sheep, pigs and horses were grazed on heathland and local people collected gorse, scrub and turfs from the heath to use as fuel. This, the grazing, and more recently controlled burning, has stopped heathland becoming woodland.

Today, man's activities are threatening the remaining heaths. Many are near built up areas and, as towns get bigger, new houses are often built on heathland. There are more and more cars and more roads are being built. Many go straight through chunks of heathland. It might not seem as though much habitat is lost, but what is left of our heathland is cut up into smaller and smaller pieces. We know that some species need big, unbroken areas and they cannot survive on small patches of heath.

Some heaths have been turned into forestry plantations and others into poor quality farmland. Traditional grazing and burning are not as common as they used to be and so many heaths are in danger of being invaded by birch or pine and losing their heathland characteristics.

If we want to see Dartford warblers, smooth snakes and sand lizards we have to make sure that there is a future for heaths.

There is some good news - conservationists are turning some areas back into heathland. You can find out more on page 44.

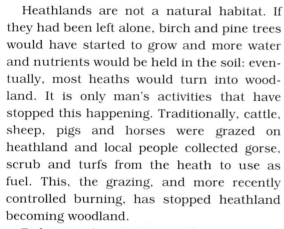

FALLING FORESTS

Half of all the world's plant and animal species are found in tropical forests. The forests contain over 2,500 bird species and yet they cover only 5 per cent of the Earth's land surface. Tropical forests are one of the most threatened habitats in the world. Every time an area of forest is cleared, species which have not even been discovered could be lost forever.

Tropical forests are found in hot, humid areas around the equator. Every month, 10 cm of rain falls and the temperature rarely drops below 20°C. With plenty of water and plenty of warmth the conditions are ideal for life, and plants and animals thrive. In Britain, 35 species of tree occur naturally, but in one acre of tropical forest there can be 250 species of tree. And, on just one tropical forest tree, there could be 350 other plant species growing.

The tropical forest is a green city. The tallest trees tower 50 m high to catch the energy pouring out of the sun. Beneath them, layer after layer of leaves of every shape and size make the most of any sunlight that gets through the canopy. Only 1 per cent of the light that hits the canopy makes it to the ground. Outside, the forest is drenched in sunlight: inside, it is cooler, still, humid and dark. Very few plants grow on the ground and most of the soil is bare.

The forest web

There are many plant and animal species in the rainforest, but surprisingly there are few individuals of each.

If you go birdwatching in Britain, you are likely to see many individual birds from a few different species, but in a tropical forest you would see just one or two birds from many different species.

Forest plants and animals depend on each other and are linked together in many ways. Here are some examples:

■ Antbirds and ant-thrushes follow marching army ants – they catch and eat the animals that run for cover as the ants approach.

■ There are forest flowers that can only be pollinated by a particular bird or bat species, and some have seeds that will not grow unless they have been right through a bird's gut.

■ Some birds use the webs of forest spiders to support their nests and they line them with forest grasses.

The forest web is very complex: biologists once thought that it was strong and able to cope with change. Now we know that it is very fragile. If one species of spider is lost, we could lose the bird that uses its web; lose the bird and we could lose a plant which needs that bird to spread its seeds; lose the plant and some insects could disappear; lose those insects and ...

A future for tropical forests?

Despite their immense beauty and obvious value, rainforests are being damaged or destroyed at alarming rates. Large areas are cleared in Central and South America to make space for cattle ranches; there is oil in

Every minute, 38 hectares of forest are destroyed. That is the same size as 45 football pitches.

Amazonia which the oil companies want; other areas are destroyed as hydroelectric dams are built; and, in Asia, huge areas are flattened for just a few logs.

According to the World Wide Fund for Nature, 20 million hectares are damaged or destroyed every year, more than twice the size of Austria.

Why are forests important?

■ The rain forests are the worlds 'lungs'. They convert huge amounts of carbon dioxide into oxygen. Without them the greenhouse effect would accelerate. Sea levels could rise, crops could fail and weather patterns change.

■ Pineapples, bananas, coffee and cocoa are some of the foods which come from tropical forests. Some forest plants have been used to increase the resistance of crops to

disease and over 2,000 plants from tropical forests have anti-cancer properties.

■ Forests produce timber, rubber, flavourings and dyes.

If we destroy the forests we will lose food, medicines and other valuable materials before they are even discovered.

The resplendent quetzal

The resplendent quetzal (pronounced ket-saal) is thought by some to be the most beautiful bird in the world. The male is stunning green and red and his tail is 65 cm long!

Resplendent quetzals are found from Mexico to Panama in high altitude forest called cloud forest. The species is protected by law in Mexico, Costa Rica and Panama and is the national bird of Guatemala.

Despite this, quetzals are at risk. Cattle ranches, coffee plantations and lots of small scale farms are destroying their cloud forest home and, because of their beauty, they are hunted for their feathers, for pets and to sell to collectors. Quetzals are not the rarest bird in the cloud forest, but if the cloud forest is lost, so too is the quetzal, and much more.

The white-necked picathartes

Imagine a dark cave in a West African forest: this is the home of a remarkable bird, the white-necked picathartes. This

The resplendent quetzal (top) lives in cloud forest in Central America. The white-necked picathartes, (above) a rare bird of West African forests.

KEY

■ Existing rainforest

■ Former areas of rainforest

Where are the world's tropical forests? Over half are in Central and South America. South-east Asia and central Africa are important forest areas, too.

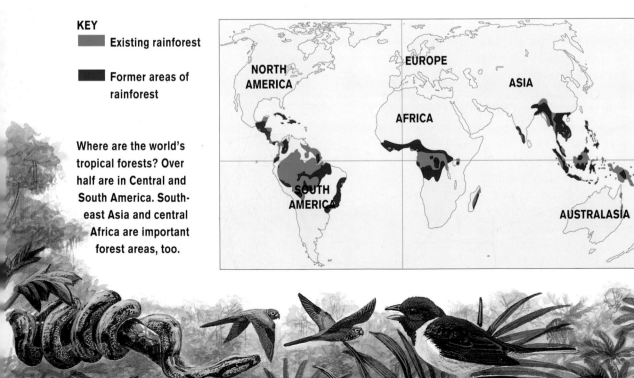

NORTH AMERICA

EUROPE

ASIA

AFRICA

SOUTH AMERICA

AUSTRALASIA

unusual bird eats beetles, cockroaches, grasshoppers, ants and other insects. It builds two nests – one for breeding and one for roosting – from mud and hangs them on a rock face inside a cave.

Two thirds of West Africa's rainforest has been lost. Farming, logging and collecting fuel-wood are all eating away at the forest, but there are other problems for picathartes – they are still hunted for food and collected for zoos. Many die within a day of being caught and those that survive may live just a few years in a faraway zoo. At one time it was thought that captive breeding could save the species, but they rarely breed successfully in zoos.

If the picathartes is to survive, it must be properly protected. In most of West Africa it is still not protected by law. Most importantly, its forest habitat must be saved.

The RSPB is trying to save the picathartes in Sierra Leone. Part of the plan is to persuade tourists to visit Sierra Leone to see its wildlife. The hope is that local people and the government will be able to make money from the forest and the picathartes and its forest home would then be a lot more secure.

DOES IT MATTER?

Over the centuries many plants and animals have become extinct. Life has carried on and there are still at least 10 million species left. So does it really matter if more disappear?

The dodo once lived on Mauritius and has not been seen alive since the 1680's. Has this really made a big difference to anyone?

Scientists recently noticed that one species of tree on Mauritius was not doing too well. There were still some old trees, but few new ones growing. Eventually, they worked out why. The seeds of this tree would only grow if they had been through a dodo's digestive system! As there are no more dodos, the tree has a problem. Scientists are now working hard to save the tree species.

When just one species is lost, there can be many knock-on effects. The natural world is linked in many ways. Every species, including man, depends on other species – perhaps for food, or for a nesting place, or to distribute seeds. This forms a very complicated web, linking many plants and animals. If one part of the web is removed it affects every other part of the web.

The natural world has provided us with food, medicines and many other useful products. Just three species of grass – rice, wheat and corn – provide the main foods for humans all over the world. Every plant and animal that we eat today originally came from a wild species.

Tribal people throughout the world have used plants to cure illnesses for thousands of years. Navajo Indian medicine men in North America used nearly 200 plant species to cure their patients! This century, doctors have realised that many of these cures work. Modern birth control pills are based on a chemical found in yams and a substance found in foxgloves was the model for a drug that is still used to treat heart disease. A new drug, 'Taxol', is used to treat cancer. It comes from the bark of an American yew tree.

These are just a few examples of how the natural world has helped mankind. Every time a species is lost we simply don't know what we are losing – it could be an important new food or a life-saving drug.

This oak tree web is just one example of how life on earth is connected. If one part of the web disappears, what is left becomes weaker.

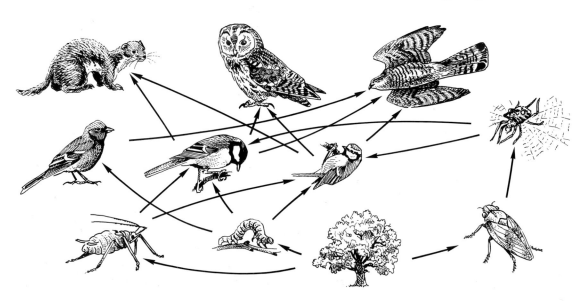

Cinchona trees (above) come from the Andes in South America. Their bark is a source of quinine, which is used to treat malaria.

Wildlife brings huge amounts of pleasure to lots of people. There are beautiful birds, weird birds, fascinating birds and record-breaking birds. They live in strange places and do amazing things. This alone is an extremely good reason to make sure that they are protected.

A rivetting story

It is the first day of your holiday and you are about to climb the steps to get into the aeroplane. Suddenly, you notice a man crawling around on one of the plane's wings!

When you take a closer look, you see that he has a big pair of pliers and is doing something to the wing. You ask him what he's doing. 'Don't worry,' he says, 'I'm just taking a few of the rivets out of the wing – the airline sells them and gets three pounds for each one!' You are very worried. After all, if some of the rivets are missing the wing might fall off! 'What if the wing falls off?' you shout. 'Don't worry,' the man with the pliers replies, 'We've been taking out a few rivets every now and then for years, and it hasn't fallen off

Most of the world's food comes from just three species of grass, including corn (top). Yams (above) are an important food for many people. They are also the chemical basis of modern birth control pills.
This yew tree (right) could save lives. A new anti-cancer drug has been discovered in its bark.

yet. It's perfectly safe – I'm travelling on this flight, too, so I wouldn't be doing it if there was any danger.'

When a species becomes extinct, it is a bit like a rivet being pulled out of plane's wing. A lot of the rivets don't seem to have any great effect on the strength of the wing, but the more rivets you remove, the weaker the wing gets, and sooner or later ...

(Story based on 'The rivet poppers' from *Extinction* by Paul and Anne Ehrlich.)

WARNING LIGHTS

Birds are easy to see and are watched by a lot of people. This, and the fact that they are found almost everywhere, makes them excellent early warning systems. Birds often provide the first sign that something is wrong in the natural world. Their numbers may drop or their behaviour may change – hopefully someone will notice before it's too late.

Birds are just one part of the web of life, and when they face problems, other parts of the web do too. Some of the signs are easy to read. You don't need to be a genius to work out what's gone wrong when seabirds are washed up dead covered in heavy oil. In the last few decades there have been many examples of birds telling us that we are not looking after the planet properly.

■ In 1960, the RSPB was getting reports of sightings of many dead birds. When the bodies were examined by scientists they found that all of them had been killed by pesticides. The following year, there were more poisonings: 600 birds died on one estate in Norfolk and in

The ups and downs of the peregrine population.

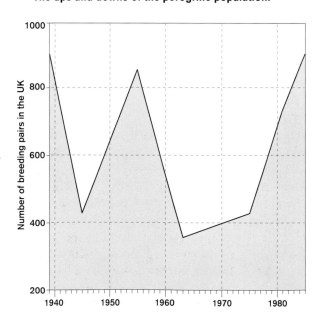

Lincolnshire 10,000 birds died. One witness said, 'pigeons are suddenly dropping out of the sky, dead'. At the time there were only two scientists in the country who were able to examine the bodies and work out what had killed them. This was a warning light letting us know how dangerous pesticides could be.

■ A warning light shone very brightly in the Irish sea in 1969 when 17,000 dead seabirds were found. They were not covered in oil and there was no obvious cause of death. When their bodies were examined, scientists found large amounts of chemicals called PCB's. PCB's were used to make paints and plastics and had been leaking into rivers and seas for years. Today, PCB's are thought to be a health hazard to people as well as wildlife and are used much less than they used to be.

■ In Sweden, mercury from paper mills was killing white-tailed eagles. The mercury was poisoning the fish that the eagles ate and was eventually killing the birds. Another warning light had been switched on and now there are controls to protect Sweden's wildlife from mercury pollution.

■ The fumes from power stations and cars dissolve in rain making acid rain. When it falls, acid rain poisons lakes and forests. Birds could be a useful warning light for acid rain – in Canada, great northern divers have stopped breeding on lakes polluted with acid rain.

The peregrine's story

The story of the peregrine is one of the best examples of a warning light. During World War II, homing pigeons were used to carry messages. Because peregrines may have eaten these pigeons, stopping important messages getting through, many adults were shot and nests and eggs destroyed. Before the war there were 900 pairs of peregrines in Britain: at the end of the war the number had been cut in half. It took ten years for the numbers to build up.

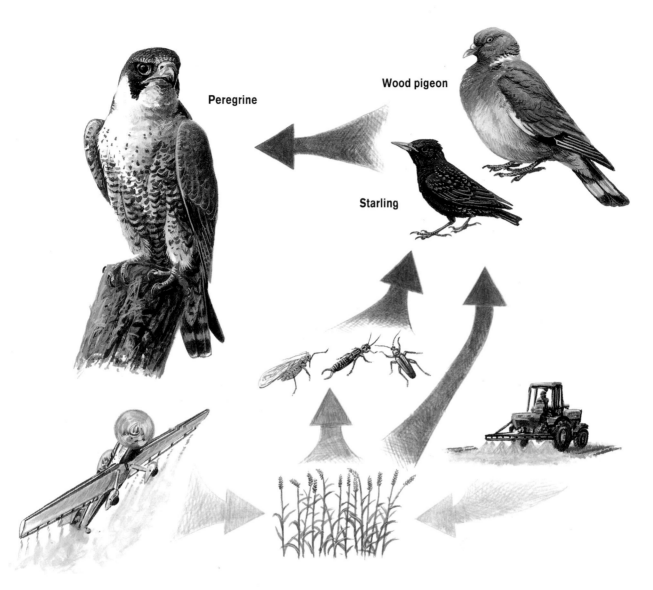

Peregrine

Wood pigeon

Starling

The warning light came on in 1961 when the peregrine was in serious trouble. Everywhere, their numbers were down and, in 1963, there were only 360 pairs.

Farmers had been using new chemicals to protect their crops from insect pests. One of these chemicals was dieldrin. It killed the insects but it also killed birds that ate the grain. Some of the grain-eating birds survived, carrying the poison in their bodies. Sparrowhawks, kestrels, tawny owls, barn owls and little owls were found dead around fields where dieldrin was used. Foxes died, too, because they ate the bodies of birds that had been killed by the poison.

Chemicals sprayed on crops to kill insect pests work their way up the food chain. The peregrine is at the top of this food chain and that is where the poisons end up.

Pigeons, thrushes, starlings and other small birds which survived the poisoning were deadly. Peregrines ate these birds and the poisons moved up the food chain, building up in peregrines. Many died and those that survived laid eggs with shells so thin that when the adult bird sat on them, the eggs broke. If the eggs got as far as hatching, most chicks soon died. Dieldrin was finally banned as a crop insecticide in 1975.

When farmers stopped using the chemicals, peregrine numbers went up. Today, the British population is very healthy.

The shrike's story

Not all changes in bird populations are the fault of humans. Red-backed shrikes used to breed all over Britain; on waste ground, in wild overgrown hedges, on heathland, and in almost any shrubby area.

The population has been falling since the middle of the last century. Red-backed shrikes were quite common 50 years ago, but by the 1980's the only birds left were found in East Anglia. In 1987 and 1988, only one or two pairs bred and in 1989 they were extinct as a breeding bird in Britain.

Ornithologists are not sure why shrikes no longer breed in Britain, but they do not believe that humans were the main problem. Most blame the weather! British weather patterns have been gradually changing and somehow, but nobody has worked out how, this has cut down the amount of food available for shrikes. There are other theories:

some people think that changes in farming methods may be partly to blame or that pesticides reduced the amount of food in the food web. No one knows for sure.

While humans were probably not the main problem facing the shrike in Britain, they did play a part. Egg-collecting is against the law but some people still do it. When a bird is in danger of dying out, egg-collecting is a very big threat. There would probably still be a few shrikes in Britain today if their eggs had not been stolen. One particular egg-collector made very careful notes of all of the red-backed shrike eggs he had stolen. During his lifetime, he stole at least 175 clutches: a total of 884 eggs. Why? All he had in his cabinet was 884 hollow, empty lumps of calcium. If he had left the eggs in their nests, that would have been another 884 chances for the red-backed shrike.

The decline of the red-backed shrike in Britain. Unlike the peregrine population, red-backed shrikes have not recovered.

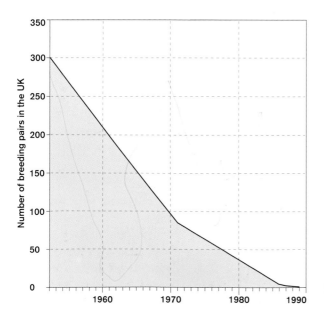

The Arctic tern, a true global traveller. In the late 1980s, food shortages caused serious problems for Arctic terns nesting in Britain.

A tern for the better ...

Arctic terns are world-wide travellers. Their Arctic to Antarctic migration is a round trip of 22,000 miles and is the longest migration of any animal.

A few years ago, Arctic terns came close to a major catastrophe. In 1980, 75,000 pairs bred in Britain – that was a third of all the Arctic terns which bred in north-west Europe. A few of these terns bred in England and Wales but most – 65,000 of them – bred on just two groups of islands off the north coast of Scotland: the Orkneys and the Shetlands.

Arctic terns nest on the ground in colonies containing as many as 10,000 pairs of birds. The adults and the chicks eat small fish, especially sandeels. In 1984, ornithologists noticed that fewer Arctic terns were breeding in the Shetlands.

Over the next six years the numbers got smaller and smaller. To make matters worse, the Arctic terns which did manage to breed were raising fewer young.

The situation got worse and worse until hardly any Arctic tern chicks were surviving. The numbers of other breeding seabirds in the area were falling, too. By 1989, the number of Arctic terns was dangerously low, only a third of what it was in 1980. The warning light was on. Something, somewhere, was seriously wrong. At about the same time, the Shetlands sandeel fishery was having problems. (Sandeels are tiny fish which are caught to be used in fertilisers, pet food or fish food. They are not caught to be eaten by people). The sandeel catch was getting smaller and smaller. Man was competing with wildlife for the fish and there simply weren't enough to go round.

Nobody knows what caused the number of sandeels to drop. It could have been part of a natural cycle, it could have been caused by the sandeel fishery taking too many fish out of the sea for too many years, it could have been a bit of both. Whatever the reason, industrial fishing for sandeels was not helping Arctic terns.

For years the sandeel fishery had been told to take fewer fish out of the sea. In 1989, they finally took notice and, in 1991, the fishery was closed. That same year, Arctic terns bred successfully for the first time since 1983. The fishery was closed again in 1992, when the terns bred successfully and other seabirds numbers started to recover.

Birds like the Arctic tern can be very good warning lights. But when the warning lights come on, we have to see them and take the right action before it is too late. If we do this, the future should be a lot brighter for birds.

R*ED DATA BIRDS*

One in nine of the world's bird species could be facing global extinction. That's over 1100 species and they are all listed in the Red Data Book. The Red Data Book is a very important document because It tells governments and conservationists that over 1100 warning lights are flashing around the world. Birds cannot survive on their own so the warning lights tell us that many other animals and plants must be at risk, too.

Noisy bustards

Bustards look like a cross between an ostrich and a turkey! They live in open areas and are very, very shy. The Bengal florican is a bustard which lives in Asia. There are probably less than 400 of them and they are found mainly in Nepal and India.

Bustards are well known for their incredible courtship displays, and the Bengal florican is no exception. The male displays early in the morning or at the end of the day. He

does something that any female bustard in the area can't fail to notice. He leaps straight up, to a height of four metres, with his shiny, black head and neck feathers puffed out, and floats back down to the ground like a ball being blown around in the wind. And, just in case any females are looking the wrong way, he makes a lot of noise – as he leaps, he claps his bright white wings together so loudly that the noise can be heard half a mile away! When the day warms up, he heads off into areas with longer grass, sometimes 10 m long. So, unless you are lucky enough to see one displaying, it is very hard to find a Bengal florican.

The problem facing the florican is that there is less suitable grassland than there used to be. A lot of it has been turned into farmland. India suffers from some of the worst food shortages in the world and local people have to grow food to survive. However, not all of the new farmland is growing food for local people. Some of it is growing cash crops such as sugar, cotton and peanuts, which are sold to help India pay its debts to other countries. In the developing world, conservation problems are sometimes very complicated with no easy solution. Thankfully, Nepal has a

This could be the best view you will ever have of a Bengal florican. They are shy, there aren't many left and you would have to travel a long way to see one.

number of national parks and reserves where Bengal Floricans are well protected.

There are two types of bustard in Western Europe: the great bustard and the little bustard. They have many things in common with their Asian cousin, including the fact that they, too, are at risk.

A mountain top grebe

The Andes is one of the world's great mountain ranges running almost the whole length of South America. They are home to the world's heaviest flying bird, the Andean condor, and a very rare flightless bird, the Junin grebe. Junin grebes are found only on Lake Junin, a shallow lake 4000 metres above sea level. Junin grebes cannot fly and have very small flight muscles. This means that there isn't much meat on a Junin grebe and they are not hunted for food.

Just 50 years ago, ornithologists described them as very, very common. Thirty years ago they were still common. But, 25 years ago the lake turned red when it was polluted by local copper, zinc and silver mines. In one year, a third of all of the life in the lake was destroyed. By 1993, only 50 Junin grebes were left. The grebes face other problems, too. In 1992 a drought made the pollution even worse, and made it easy for dogs, foxes and rats to eat the grebes' eggs and young.

But there is hope for the Junin grebe. Conservationists are looking for a similar lake in the area to move some of the birds to. And there are plans to turn Lake Junin into a reservoir for Lima, the capital of Peru. If this happens, the water will have to be cleaned up and that could save the Junin grebe. Normally, conservationists would be against this development but the lake has already been so badly damaged, this is probably the best solution.

How many birds are at risk?

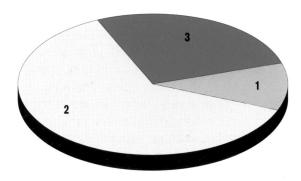

1. Red data species 11%
2. Going down 62%
3. Birds that are safe, and birds that we do not have enough information about to know 27%

Too many birds are at risk. Over 70 per cent are declining, including many that could disappear forever.

WHAT ARE THE THREATS?

■ **Habitat loss**
The biggest threat to the world's birdlife. Over 60 per cent of birds at risk are threatened by habitat loss.

■ **Hunting, egg-collecting and poisoning**
A problem for one-third of the world's threatened birds.

■ **The wild bird trade**
Over 40 species are threatened by the trade, including 30 types of parrot.

■ **Introduced species**
Introduce a species to an area where it does not normally live and there are often problems.

■ **Pollution**
Nobody knows what impact acid rain and the greenhouse effect will have on birds. Pollution from farms and factories all cause problems for wildlife.

RARE BIRDS IN EUROPE

You don't have to travel to South America or Asia to find threatened birds. There are 24 Red Data species in Europe. There were 26, but the Canary Island black oystercatcher and the bald ibis have since become extinct in Europe.

Corncrake crisis

The corncrake is one of the three Red Data birds in Britain. It is a plain grey-brownish crake that spends most of its time in thick vegetation. They are hard to see, but easy to

There are very few corncrakes left. Bird trappers in North Africa are one of the threats they face.

hear. Their call is unmistakeable and so loud that it can be heard nearly a mile away.

This bird is named after its call – the corncrake's scientific name is *Crex crex*, which is a good description of the noise it makes. It is hard to describe bird noises on paper but the corncrake sounds a bit like a piece of wood being scraped across a notched piece of wood. People who have not heard a corncrake, instantly know what it is when they hear it! Corncrakes call mainly at night and there are reports of people being kept awake by the sound.

A hundred years ago, corncrakes were common birds in meadows all over lowland Europe. Only 50 years ago, their rasping calls were still quite common in many parts of England. But, since the 1950's, the number of corncrakes has gone down and down. Now, they are found only in the Inner and Outer Hebrides and parts of Ireland. In 1978, 2200 male corncrakes did their best to keep people in Britain and Ireland awake at night; ten years later there were only 1494; five years on, in 1993, there were only 643.

Corncrakes migrate: they spend summer in Europe and winter in Zimbabwe, Malawi, and South Africa. Birds that migrate are harder to protect than birds that stay in one country all year round. There isn't much point protecting a bird in Britain if the main threats to its survival are in another country. Birds need to be protected everywhere. But to make things complicated, corncrakes use two different migration routes. In the spring, when they travel from Africa to Europe, they go via Morocco. In the autumn, when they head south, they go through Egypt.

Migrating corncrakes have two main hazards to cope with. Travelling through Egypt is especially risky because bird trappers put out nets to catch quails, and they end up catching corncrakes, too. We don't know how many corncrakes are killed in Egypt's quail nets; it could be 200 a year or 2000. Others are killed because they fly into lighthouses and overhead wires.

However, the main threat to the corncrake is in Europe, where they breed. Corncrakes nest on the ground in tall plants. In the early part of the breeding season they often use iris beds, patches of reeds and clumps of stinging nettles and, later, when the grass is long enough, they breed in hay meadows.

As for many other species, habitat loss is the main threat to the corncrake's survival. Some hay meadows have been turned into silage fields where the hay is cut two or three times a year and the cut grass is stored to be used for cattle food in the winter. And, because the field is cut early in the season, corncrake nests, chicks and sometimes adults are destroyed.

In other places, there are more sheep than there used to be and the grass is grazed so much that it is too short to provide enough cover for nesting corncrakes. Modern machinery and mowing methods also cause problems because they trap corncrakes in fields giving them no escape route.

Where are the world's threatened birds?

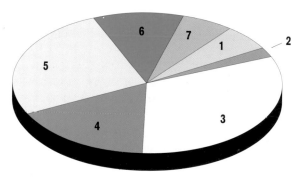

1. 6% are in Europe, Russia and the Middle East
2. 2% are in North America
3. 32% are in Central and South America
4. 17% are in Africa
5. 26% are in Asia
6. 11% are in Australia, New Zealand and New Guinea
7. 6% are in Pacific Ocean Island

The RSPB is doing everything it can to save the corncrake. Farmers are being encouraged to change the way they mow their fields so that corncrakes have a chance to get away from the mowing machine. The government is also paying farmers to mow their fields at the end of the season when the corncrakes have finished nesting.

Today, less land is being farmed, and corncrakes are starting to appear on areas that have been set aside.

The red kite

Red kites were once a common sight in lowland Britain: they were even a common sight in London and were protected by a royal law. But, in the 1400's, people started poisoning, shooting and trapping them and by 1879 only a few pairs were left. In the 1930's, they were nearly extinct in Britain.

A few red kites, however, survived in wild, remote places in Central Wales, and their numbers have been slowly building up. Egg-collectors have caused red kites a lot of problems, and the species would not have survived in Wales if the nests had not been guarded around the clock. Recently, the army has helped the RSPB to guard the nests and, in 1993, only one clutch was stolen. Welsh kites are now doing well: over 100 pairs bred in 1994.

The Welsh population may be doing well, but there are no signs that it will spread into England and Scotland where red kites used to be common.

So, in 1989, conservationists decided to bring red kites back to England and Scotland. Reintroducing a bird to an area

The red kite reintroduction project is working well. Red kites are breeding once again in England and Scotland.

where it used to be found is very different to introducing a bird to a place where it does not normally occur (like the ruddy duck - see page 36). Conservationists have very strict controls and birds are only reintroduced into an area if:

1 We know that it used to be there.
2 We know why it disappeared.
3 The problems that made it disappear have been sorted out.
4 There is enough suitable habitat left.
5 The population that the new birds will be taken from will not be harmed.

Secret sites, military planes and electronic wizardry

Nests were selected in Sweden and Spain and chicks were taken only from nests with two or more young in. The young kites were then rushed to Britain by the RAF and British Airways. After five weeks in special aviaries, where the young kites continued to grow and learned to feed themselves, they were released in top secret sites in England and Scotland.

All of the red kites were fitted with plastic wing tags and tiny radio transmitters on their tails. The wing tags would help ornithologists to identify individual kites if they could read the letters or numbers on the tag. Scientists used the transmitters to follow the kites' movements after their release.

Since the scheme began, over 150 red kites have been released in Scotland and England. Most are still alive, but some have died. At least five have been illegally poisoned.

In 1992, for the first time in over 100 years, a pair of red kites bred in Scotland and several pairs bred in England! In 1994, there were nearly 30 pairs of red kites breeding in England and Scotland, and they were raising young successfully. Hopefully, the red kite is back for good, but it will be some years before we can be absolutely sure. In the meantime, watch out for red kites – they fly long distances so you could see one almost anywhere!

GOOD NEWS: In 1994 the red kite was taken off the world red data list.

THE DALMATIAN PELICAN

The Dalmatian pelican is the world's biggest pelican and a global Red Data bird. There are only about 20 places where they still breed, and there are only about 1200 pairs left in Europe. The Danube Delta in Romania is one of Europe's most important wetlands and Dalmatian pelicans still breed there. But the pelican and the Delta are struggling. Marshes have been drained and turned into farmland and there is a pollution problem. To make things worse for the pelicans, local fishermen think they take too many fish, so adult birds are shot. The Delta and the pelicans have to be saved.

Battle of the stifftails

There are nine species of stifftails (a type of duck) in the world. All of them dive and none of them spend much time on land. Not surprisingly, they have stiff tails: tails that can be laid flat in the water or held up straight in the air.

The white-headed duck is the only stifftail found naturally in the whole of Europe, North Africa and Asia, and in the last 100 years it has had a tough time. Nobody knows how many there used to be, but in the 1930's 47,000 were counted on the Caspian Sea. Today, there are only 19,000 in the world and under 800 in western Europe. The European birds live in Spain. They used to breed in Corsica, Italy, Greece, Albania, Morocco, Israel, Egypt and Hungary, but not any more.

Earlier this century, habitat loss, hunting and egg-collecting were the big problems. In 1977 there were only 22 white-headed ducks left in Spain on just three lakes. With a lot of hard work by Spanish conservationists the species was rescued and 15 years later there were 790. It is a globally threatened bird and the species now faces a new threat, one that nobody expected.

The ruddy duck is a common North American bird. It is not a threatened species: there are 650,000 of them in the wild in North America and Canada. Ruddy ducks are not native to Europe. In 1950, there were none in the wild in Europe, but there were a few in wildfowl collections. When ruddy ducks escaped from wildfowl collections in Britain most birdwatchers were pleased to add another bird to their lists. But the ruddy ducks have been very successful – the population has grown and is spreading. Today, there are thousands and they are threatening the existence of the white-headed duck.

Because they are so closely related, male ruddy ducks can mate with female white-headed ducks. Ruddy ducks are more aggressive birds and they drive male white-headed ducks out of their territories. This problem would not have occurred if ruddy ducks had not been brought over to Europe – they would be thousands of miles away in North America.

When two different species breed together, the offspring (called hybrids) are normally sterile. This means that when they are adults, they are unable to produce young. But the ruddy duck and white-headed duck hybrids in Spain are fertile; when they become adults, they produce young.

Unless something is done quickly, all of the excellent work that helped the white-headed duck survive this long will have been

Ruddy ducks. Handsome and harmless? In North America, maybe, but not in Europe.

a waste of time and there will be no pure white-headed ducks left in Western Europe. The ruddy duck has reached Morocco. If it continues to spread, it will reach Turkey and Asia where other white-headed ducks breed.

In 1992, ruddy ducks and hybrids were shot in Spain to protect the white-headed duck population. The shooting will probably have to continue for some time to give the white-headed duck a chance to survive. Action will need to be taken in other countries, too, or more and more ruddy ducks will arrive in Spain. Ornithologists do not like having to kill one bird to protect another, especially when there would not have been a problem if the birds had not been introduced in the first place.

To introduce or not to introduce ...

Little owls and ring-necked parakeets were both introduced (or escaped from captivity) in Britain and neither species seems to cause any serious problems.

But often, introduced species do cause problems. When mallards were introduced to New Zealand they did exactly the same thing to New Zealand black ducks as ruddy ducks are beginning to do to white-headed ducks. Now there are very few New Zealand black ducks left. Perhaps it would be safer not to introduce birds to new countries.

But the Mandarin duck might make you think again. Mandarin ducks escaped from collections and there are now perhaps 1000 living in the wild in Britain. In China and Japan, where they live naturally, their numbers are going down fast. The British population could become the world stronghold, and perhaps even save the Mandarin duck from global extinction.

White-headed ducks (above) are facing a new threat from a close relative. As the map below shows, they are only found in a few places in Europe and these populations are at risk.

 Breeding areas of the white-headed duck in Europe.

GOING DOWN

Only three British bird species are threatened on a world-wide scale, but many others are declining and some could disappear from Britain forever.

'Birds to Watch 2' is the world's bird Red Data book. It lists every bird species at risk of world-wide extinction. There is also a Red Data book for the UK's birds only. A bird can get into it if:

- 15 per cent of the European population lives in the UK
- less than 300 pairs breed in the UK
- their numbers have dropped by more than a quarter in 25 years
- half of the population are at ten sites or fewer.
- the species future in Europe looks poor, or the bird is globally threatened.

Sadly, the UK red data book includes over 140 species. Over 20 are of 'critical conservation concern'. This means that urgent action is needed to protect them to make sure that they have a future in the UK. The bittern and the night-jar are both on this list.

Barn owls (above) face problems: there are fewer old barns to nest in and less rough grassland to hunt in. Black-tailed godwits (below) need wet grassland and there isn't much left.

The black-tailed godwit

This wader stopped breeding in Britain in the 1800's. In the 1950's it started again but still their numbers have been dropping. The few pairs that are left breed on very few sites. They need the right kind of wet grass-land, flooded at the right time of year, and that is hard to find.

On a global scale this species is not at serious risk, but it is threatened in Europe. So should conservationists spend time and money trying to increase the numbers in Britain? Would the money be better spent on birds that are globally threatened? These are hard questions to answer.

If we take a global view we might not worry too much because there are black-tailed godwits in other places. Maybe the fact that we enjoy seeing them is a good enough reason to protect them. And we don't know what lies ahead for the rest of Europe's black-tailed godwits. We have to make sure that birds

No-one knows exactly how many nightjars there are. But they are certainly still at risk.

The shoveler (below) seems safe at the moment, but its numbers could easily go down. It needs shallow, eutrophic (see page 12) water which means it is at risk from drainage projects. This has already happened in at least one important area – the marshes in north Kent.

are protected all the time, not just when they are about to disappear forever.

The bittern

This heron (see page 13) is very hard to see, but not just because it is well camouflaged: there are very few left. It's easier to hear a bittern than to see one – the males make a loud booming noise, a bit like a fog horn.

You count bitterns by counting the booming males – easy, or so ornithologists thought, until they realised that because the same males were covering big areas and booming from different places, they had been counted more than once. However, when the booms were recorded scientists found that each male had a unique voice pattern. They used the information to get a better idea of the numbers: in 1994, there were 16 in the UK.

The bittern could disappear from Britain soon. Pesticides, pollution, loss of habitat, and the weather have probably all caused problems for the bittern.

The nightjar

The nightjar is one of Britain's most unusual birds. It lives in Britain in summer and keeps its head down during the day. Nightjars wake up when the sun sets and insects don't know what has hit them as these birds trawl the air for a crunchy insect supper at twilight.

Many nightjars breed on heathlands, an important habitat that is under threat (see pages 18 and 19). A few years ago, bird-watchers took part in a nationwide survey to count the nightjars breeding in the UK and from the results, they thought that nightjar numbers were going up. Scientists now think the count was inaccurate, so work is still needed to save this secretive bird.

SUCCESS

So far, this book has concentrated on mostly bad news. But, there is good news, too. Some species have been saved and others have returned to areas where they used to breed. Ornithologists have even rediscovered birds that they thought were extinct.

The Seychelles magpie robin

This bird used to be common in the Seychelles; today, it is one of the world's rarest birds. In 1989, there were only about 20 left, but with BirdLife International's help it should have a future. Numbers are going up – there were 40 in 1994. With so few birds left it is important that as many chicks survive as possible, so conservationists catch cockroaches for the magpie robins to eat. The adults then don't have to spend too long away from the nest looking for food. They can make sure that their eggs and young are properly protected from predators like mynah birds.

The Gurney's pitta

This beautiful bird had not been seen in its native Thailand since 1952 and was declared extinct in 1985. In 1986, however, it was rediscovered and is now part of a BirdLife International project. To provide food and timber for local people, trees have been planted to take the

After near extinction, Seychelles magpie robins (top) are slowly building up their numbers. The Gurney's pitta (right) was rediscovered in 1986 after it was thought to be extinct! The great bustard (above) is a European bird at risk. Work to save their steppe habitat will hopefully be a success. Ospreys (opposite page) are part of a very famous success story.

pressure off the natural forest, where the pitta lives. A few tourists are visiting the area to see the wildlife and this is making money without harming the forest. If the project works, it will be good for local people and for wildlife.

The osprey

Ospreys stopped breeding in Britain in 1916. In the 1950's they returned and bred succesfully at Loch Garten in 1954. However, egg-collectors struck in 1955 and 1956 and in the following year, an osprey was shot. The RSPB decided to guard the nest and protect it from egg-collectors and, in 1959, ospreys were back. They return to breed each year and Loch Garten is now a famous RSPB nature reserve.

The cahow

The cahow is a small seabird from Bermuda. Black rats, introduced to Bermuda in 1609, ate all the cahows and no more were seen until 300 years later when one was found on a nearby island. One was seen again in 1935, and in 1945 their breeding ground was found by accident when an airforce base was being built. Today, there are only about 20, but the cahow is hanging on.

The takahe

The takahe is a flightless bird living in New Zealand. Some takahe bones were found in 1847 when it was thought to be extinct and two years later, a living takahe was caught by a dog! None were seen for 28 years, then another was caught. In 1948, nearly 50 years since a takahe was last seen, scientists thought that the bird must have become extinct. Then an expedition found three Takahes! Now the bird is protected and will hopefully be safe.

Other discoveries

■ The yellow-fronted gardener bowerbird wasn't seen alive until 1981 – it was only known to exist from a few feathers.
■ The Madagascan serpent eagle disappeared in 1930, but was found again in 1988.
■ The Madagascan pochard was found again in 1991.
■ In 1993 the four-coloured flowerpecker from the Philippines was seen for the first time in 80 years.

THE FUTURE

Humans have been destroying wildlife habitats for a long time, but we are now helping to reverse the trend. There are some important habitats that we might be able to recreate. We know that 70 per cent of the world's threatened birds live in just two per cent of the world's land surface. This means that we can make sure our efforts are directed to where they are needed most.

Bird hot spots

Madagascar is home to 250 species of birds, 150 of which breed nowhere else in the world. Places with lots of endemic species contain some of the most fragile chunks of life on the planet. (An endemic species is found in only one place.)

Ornithologists from BirdLife International have identified 221 endemic bird areas. They did this by deciding that any land bird with a range of 50,000 km^2 or less was a species with a small range (50,000 km^2 might sound a lot but it is only about a fifth of the size of Britain). A computer was used to put all of these ranges onto a map – over a quarter of the world's birds have a small range so this was a big job.

Any area with two or more of these species was classified as an endemic bird area – a bird hotspot that must be protected.

There are bird hotspots all over the world but most are in the tropics: 55 in South America and 37 in Africa. About half of the hotspots support between two and ten endemic bird species; some support over 50 endemic species.

These hotspots are important because they highlight places that need urgent protection, helping conservationists know where to spend time and money. And endemic bird areas also contain many rare plants and other threatened animals. By protecting them we will protect a big chunk of the world's threatened wildlife.

The rare hyacinth macaw is threatened by the wild bird trade. In 1990, a pair was on sale in Britain for £25,000.

Trading in wild birds

Over 2,600 different species of birds have been taken from the wild and sold as pets. Huge numbers of birds are involved in this trade: one and a half million are caught and transported to Europe every year.

The Convention on International Trade in Endangered Species (CITES) was set up to control the trade and over 120 countries around the world have agreed to follow the CITES guidelines. CITES protects over 1000 species of threatened birds. Most species can be traded, but only with a special permit and if the wild populations will not suffer as a result. Some species are so threatened that they cannot be traded.

If CITES worked, no wildlife would be at risk from international trade. Unfortunately, it doesn't. In many countries where protected species are caught it is easy to get forged documents or bribe an official to get genuine documents. Many countries' officials also ignore the part of CITES that says the trade should not damage wild populations. For example, scientists know very little about green-winged macaws and there is no way to know whether taking birds from the wild damages the population. Yet, until recently they were exported from Guyana, South America.

The world's endemic bird areas cover just two per cent of the Earth's land surface. They are vitally important areas for wildlife conservation.

The rare Goffin's cockatoo lives in Indonesia. Thousands have been traded in the last ten years, so recently, the species was given even more protection under CITES. However, bird dealers heard that this would happen and so they exported as many as they could before CITES was changed!

The wild bird trade must be controlled, but this is not easy to do. Poorer countries simply do not have the money to make CITES work. The best solution is to take away the demand for wild-caught birds – if nobody buys them, there will be no reason to take them from the wild.

Birds belong in the wild, not in a cage, but some people still want to keep birds as pets. If someone you know wants a pet bird, ask them to make sure that it was bred in captivity before they buy it.

They should never buy a bird that has been trapped, stuffed in a crate with lots of other birds and flown across the world to spend the rest of its life in a cage. Tell them that for every wild bird that makes it to a pet shop, up to four will die on the way.

Rebuilding lost habitats

An exciting experiment is taking place in a field in Suffolk where the RSPB is trying to turn farmland back into heathland. When the land was farmed, fertilizers were used on the soil so the nutrients built up. Because heathland plants need poor quality soil, the nutrients had to be taken out of the ground before heather could grow. Barley and linseed were planted, in summer and winter, for several years and these crops gradually sucked out the nutrients, leaving less and less in the soil.

Heathland plants also need just the right soil acidity. If it is too acidic or not acidic enough, the field will never become heathland. The fertilizers left huge amounts of calcium in the ground which is very hard to get out. This means that the soil had too little acid in it. Other treatments are now being used to try and change the acidity.

When the soil is just right, heathland plants may spread into the area naturally or they might need to be planted. If the experiment works, conservationists should be able

Bharatpur, India (above). Wildlife tourism could help save this superb wetland.
In Suffolk, (above right), the RSPB is turning farmland into heathland.
Young people can make a difference – children in Ghana (below right) have played a big part in conserving the roseate tern.

to create new heathlands elsewhere.

New reedbeds are also being created. If the water quality is right, this is not too difficult because reedbeds form naturally, but often conservationists need to lend a helping hand and plant clumps of reeds in the water. The new reedbeds are doing well and should help rare birds like the bittern (see page 13).

The world in your hands

You may know how hard it is to change the way people think. Often, it is adults that cause problems for wildlife, and sometimes they refuse to change. But young people are more likely to change and can play a very important part in helping to protect wildlife.

In Malta, shooting is a strong tradition

children were catching them for fun. To change this, wildlife clubs were set up to teach local children to enjoy and protect their wildlife, not catch it. Today, there are nearly 200 wildlife clubs in Ghana, most of them along the coast, and tern trapping is getting rarer. Luckily the roseate tern isn't! Tern numbers have stopped going down and should soon be going up.

Making money from wildlife

If tourists pay to go somewhere because of the wildlife, there is a good chance that the country's people will look after their wildlife and the money from tourists could help conservation projects. But wildlife tourism has to be handled carefully. If there are too many tourists the wild places could be damaged or the wildlife disturbed. It is also very important that local people benefit from tourism. If all the money goes to the country's government, why should local people protect the habitat? For some places, wildlife tourism could be an important key to their conservation in the future.

A global partnership

BirdLife International, a worldwide partnership of bird conservation organisations, was launched in March 1993. It is a massive voice for wildlife, and means that the world's experts will be working together to protect birds and the places they depend on.

How you can help

There is not enough space in this book to tell you about all the things you can do to help birds. But, if you haven't already done it, you should join the YOC. The YOC is the biggest wildlife club for young people in the world.

It is the junior section of The Royal Society for the Protection of Birds (RSPB), so when you join you will add your name to hundreds of thousands of people who are doing something positive for wildlife. And, because the RSPB is the UK partner of BirdLife International, you will be part of that, too.

and thousands of birds are shot every year. There are similar problems in France and Italy, too. The Malta Ornithological Society (MOS) wants to stop the shooting, but is finding it very difficult. Young people could be the answer. MOS has put a lot of effort into helping young people understand why wildlife should be protected. So, in 20 years time, when today's young people are adults, Malta could be a very different place.

Children are part of the answer for the roseate tern, too. This species was struggling to survive and nobody could work out why. Ornithologists then discovered that the terns spend the winter in West Africa where local

CAPTIONS

Here are the names of the creatures which appear on the large illustrations in the book:

Pages 8 and 9
Garden birds, left to right:
A great spotted woodpecker, a blackbird, fieldfares, a redwing, starlings, a siskin, a greenfinch, a robin, house sparrows, a chaffinch, a collared dove, a blue tit and a great tit.

Pages 16 and 17
Estuary birds, left to right,:
A knot, a bar-tailed godwit, a dunlin, an oystercatcher, a redshank, a curlew, a shelduck and a grey heron.

Pages 20 and 21
Amazon rainforest (Ecuador), top left to bottom right:
A harpy eagle, a collared trogon, a three-toed sloth, a scarlet macaw, a plum-throated cotinga, a blue morpho butterfly, a swallow-winged puffbird, red-bellied macaws, blue and yellow macaws, a jaguar and a many-banded aracari.

Pages 22 and 23
More Amazon rainforest, bottom left to top right, anti-clockwise:
A boa, maroon-tailed parakeets, a red-capped cardinal, a violaceous jay, a ringed kingfisher, an anhinga, black skimmers, terrapins, a cayman, a white-banded swallow, a hoatzin, a white-throated toucan, a black caracara, a howler monkey and a king vulture.

INDEX

The photographs are copyright and are reproduced by kind permission of:

p.4 Bill Oddie; p.5 Dave Chandler; p.7 C H Gomersall (RSPB); p.9 (right) Reed International Books Ltd (Mike Busselles); p.9 (left) C H Gomersall (RSPB); p.10 Paul Sterry (Nature Photographers Limited); p.12 George McCarthy (RSPB); p.16 C H Gomersall (RSPB); p.19 (left) C H Gomersall (RSPB); p.19 (right) Robin Bush (Nature Photographers Ltd); p. 21 Julian Evans; p.22 (top) Michael and Patricia Fogden; p.22 (bottom) Norman Tomalin (Bruce Coleman Ltd); p.32 S Bahaeldin (BirdLife International); p.34 C H Gomersall (RSPB); p.38 W S Paton (Nature Photographers Ltd); p.40 (top) Jeff Watson (Nature Photographers Ltd); p.40 (bottom) Kevin Carlson (Nature Photographers Ltd); p.44 Judy Todd; p.45 (top and bottom) C H Gomersall (RSPB)